NO EXCUSES
MINDSET

MASTERMIND EDITION

NO EXCUSES MINDSET

MASTERMIND EDITION

WORKBOOK

FARSHAD ASL
LIVE WITH PASSION

TOPLeaders

Copyright © 2016 by Top Leaders Inc.

All rights reserved. This book or any portion thereof may not be reproduced or used in any manner whatsoever without the express written permission of the publisher except for the use of brief quotations in a book review or scholarly journal.

First Printing: 2016

Library of Congress Cataloging-in-Publication Data is available upon request.

Softcover ISBN: 978-1539893356

Printed in the United States of America
Published by Top Leaders Inc.

Ordering Information: Special discounts are available on quantity purchases by corporations, associations, educators, and others.
For more details find us at **www.Topleaders.co**

Table of Contents

A Note from Farshad Asl vii

Acknowledgements ix

Introducing the *No Excuses* Mastermind xi

The *No Excuses* Mastermind Journey xiii

The *No Excuses* Mastermind A Note to Myself xvii

My **Mission Statement** and **My Core Values** xix

My *No Excuses* Mastermind Support Team xxi

Chapter 1: **In Plain Sight** 3

Chapter 2: **Renovating the Mind** 9

Chapter 3: **Coaching** 15

Chapter 4: *No Excuses* – **Personal Growth** 21

Chapter 5: *No Excuses* – **Relationships** 27

Chapter 6: *No Excuses* – **Family** 33

Chapter 7: *No Excuses* – **Business** 39

Chapter 8: *No Excuses* – **Legacy** 45

Farshad's Mission Statement and Farshad's Core Values 49

Positive Goals 51

A Note from Farshad Asl

Congratulations on starting your *No Excuses Mindset* journey!

First and foremost, I would like to applaud you for pursuing a life of **No Excuses**. You have risen beyond being inspired and have become **intentional** about your life. Intentional living is the only way to live with a *No Excuses Mindset*.

Now that you have read *The 'No Excuses' Mindset,* you are ready to turn your knowledge into insight and turn your dreams into reality. With this Mastermind you will be able to find the success and significance you dream of and desire for.

In the early 1900's, Napoleon Hill formally introduced the concept of the Mastermind Group. Derived from his book, *"Think and Grow Rich,"* Hill wrote about the Mastermind principle as "The coordination of knowledge and effort of two or more people, who work toward a definite purpose, in the spirit of harmony."

This mastermind seeks to hone in on this **definite purpose** of living life with a *No Excuses Mindset*, while attaining 20/20 clarity, and a 3D understanding of your purpose and passion in life. Through this Mastermind you will become who you are designed to be.

> *When your purpose and passion are in alignment, your work becomes your calling, your life becomes your dream, and your mindset becomes 20/20 in clarity.*

This Mastermind can be used by the entrepreneur, businessman, millennial, leader, coach, parent, student, etcetera. **The No Excuses Mindset Mastermind** is meant to be a roadmap to your success, significance, and ultimately freedom. It will help you take massive action toward your dreams and remain accountable for yourself and fellow mastermind group members.

The best ideas always come from and amongst like-minded people with similar interests who genuinely want to grow together. Through this Mastermind, you will be inspired to growly daily amongst individuals who share the intensity in passion and purpose for their lives.

I am so excited that you have chosen to continue the *No Excuses Mindset* journey that will be a life changing experience with lifelong friends. Get ready to dive in deep and submerge yourself in self-discovery.

Sincerely,

Farshad Asl

Acknowledgements

I would like to thank Ted Gray and Richard Mireles
for their valuable contributions to this Mastermind Guide.
These men have exemplified the *No Excuses Mindset.*

Introducing the *No Excuses* Mastermind

What is a mastermind group?

> *"The coordination of knowledge and effort of two or more people, who work toward a definite purpose, in the spirit of harmony."* – Napoleon Hill

- A mastermind is a small group of individuals who come together for the purpose of supporting each other in reaching their goals. The mastermind format is unique in that it uses small groups to explore and discover the ideas from a specific book or author. This mastermind will mine the depths of **The 'No Excuses' Mindset** by Farshad Asl, entrepreneur, leadership coach, and speaker.

Who should participate?

- Masterminds are for anyone and everyone who wants to grow. They may consist of people from established groups, teams, and organization or they can consist of strangers who are willing to come to together to support each other in their personal and professional **growth journeys.**

How often and for how long should mastermind groups meet?

- Masterminds can be conducted anywhere that team members are comfortable discussing their lives. It is recommended that you meet weekly for a predetermined number of weeks/meetings. While most mastermind sessions last 60-90 minutes, you have the flexibility to adjust them based on the needs of your individual group. Nevertheless, it is important to designate a certain duration for each meeting.

Who leads a mastermind group?

- Masterminds are normally facilitated by a **team leader** who assumes responsibilities for structuring the group and guiding the group discussions. Smaller teams can alternate facilitating responsibilities as the team leader if desired.

The *No Excuses* Mastermind Journey

Welcome to the *No Excuses* Mastermind journey.

This program is designed to support you in living life with the *No Excuses Mindset*. It has been designed as a companion supplement workbook for small groups as they journey through **"The 'No Excuses' Mindset."**

> *"**Change is a difficult process**. It can truly take place in an environment of **support**, **structure**, and **sacrifice**. **Support** comes from asking for help, seeking professional coaching, and surrounding yourself with the right people. **Structure** requires accountability, a follow-up system, and action. **Sacrifice** requires paying the price and getting out of your comfort zone but staying in your strength zone."* Page 27, **The "No Excuses" Mindset**

This workbook is structured to bring maximum value to you and your team. Each chapter contains the five following components:

1. **Accountability Check**

   - In the first meeting, team members will introduce themselves and briefly discuss why they have chosen to partake in the *No Excuses* Mastermind Journey.
   - Team members will discuss and hold each other accountable for one another's action plans.
   - During the first meeting a foundation of trust and comradery will be set and accountability partners, who will assist you throughout this journey and help you gain the 20/20 mindset, will be selected.
   - In the meetings for chapters 2 through chapter 8, the accountability check will provide team members with an opportunity to share their progress in honoring their commitments to their Massive Action Steps from the previous meeting.
   - The time allotted for the Accountably Check can be used for discussing the team's progress throughout the Mastermind. Shortcomings or areas of weakness can also be discussed here. As a team you are meant to grow together in both strengths and weakness.

2. **Ice Breaker**

   - This is an opening question that provides the team with an opportunity to get warmed up to the meeting's topic right after the accountability check.
   - This will be a time of open discussion and all team members will have the chance to offer their thoughts on the ice breaker question.

- Depending on the time you have available you may decide to set a time limit for each response but you may also decide to run an organic group.
- Whatever guidelines your group decides upon, it is always best to make sure that the entire team is engaged and actively participating.

3. **Round Table Topics**

    - This component consists of several questions designed to generate awareness and understanding through inquiry and team dialogue.
    - Some of these questions are posed by Farshad in the book, while others are inspired Farshad's ideals and are generated to provoke dialogue and reflection that results in growing your awareness and understanding.
    - This is an open discussion lead by the team leader; everyone should participate during the Round Table Discussions.
    - It is during this time when the best ideas will most probably be shared and growth will occur.

4. **My 3D Mental Process**

    - At the conclusion of each chapter, Farshad poses questions that are designed to support you in gaining clarity within each dimension of the 3D Mental Process.
    - The 3D Mental Process from the book has been integrated into the curriculum so that your team can provide you with coaching as you navigate your way through the process.
    - This process is designed for one individual to take the hot seat and work through the questions while being supported by his or her team.
    - Taking the hot seat is a way for you to add value to yourself as this is an actionable pathway to a 20/20 mindset.
    - Coaching your teammates through the process is a way for you to support them in their goal to live a life of with No Excuses.
    - By design this Mastermind requires that you spend more time adding value to others.
    - Working through this process takes time so it is unlikely that every team member will have the chance to take the hot seat at every meeting. However, by coaching some of your teammates through their questions, you will be better equipped to work through these questions between sessions on your own.

5. **My Massive Action Steps**

    - We believe it is important to end each 3D Mental Process with a personal call to action. Farshad says that *"it is essential to know that it is up to you to take action – sometimes massive action."*

- Once you finish the 3D Mental Process and you discover what you need to do in order to live life with No Excuses, you are encouraged to commit to taking the Massive Action Steps toward your plan for your future.
- You should take bold life changing steps. Therefore, consider limiting yourself to three massive action steps per session.
- Write them down, share them with your team, and make sure that you and your team are clear on your completion dates for each massive action step.

The *No Excuses* Mastermind
A Note to Myself

By signing this agreement, I promise to myself to honor the commitments that are listed below.

I, _____ commit to:

- Be on time for each mastermind session which will be scheduled according to the times and dates that have been established by my team members and myself. If for some reason I will be late or absent from a meeting, then I will still honor my commitment by notifying the team member ahead of time.

- Complete the assigned readings from the text prior to each mastermind meeting.

- Spend time reflecting on the 3D Mental Process prior to each mastermind meeting.

- Complete the entire *No Excuses* Mastermind Supplement Workbook.

Signature

_____

Date

_____

My Mission Statement

"My mission in life is not merely to survive, but to thrive; and to do so with some passion, some compassion, some humor, and some style." Maya Angelou

Please take some time to think about your **Mission Statement** in life and then write it down below.

My Core Values

"Core values serve as a lighthouse when the fog of life seems to leave you wandering in circles; when you encounter that moment where every decision is a tough one and no choice seems to clearly be the better choice." J. Loren Norris

Please take some time to think about your **Core Values** in life and then write it down below.

My No Excuses Mastermind Support Team

"If you want to go fast, then go alone. If you want to go far, then go with others."
– John C. Maxwell

In order to grow and begin living a life with *No Excuses*, you will need a support team. These are the people who are going to stand with you as you make the transformation from success to significance. Take some time to get to know your *No Excuses* Mastermind Support Team.

	Name	Phone #	Email
1			
2			
3			
4			
5			
6			
7			
8			
9			
10			

Chapter 1 Agenda

In Plain Sight

- Accountability Check
- Ice Breaker
- Round Table Talk
- My 3D Mental Process
- My Massive Action Steps

1. In Plain Sight

"The two most important days in your life are the day you are born and the day you find out why." – Mark Twain

Ice Breaker

In life we have all found ourselves making excuses to justify our failures. In your opinion, why are people so often willing to live a life of excuses? Why do most people come up with excuses?

Round Table Topic

"Life is a moving target. So your vision needs to be an accurate objective, to give you direction for your actions. As you move toward your goal, the vision becomes even more substantive, more palpable. It becomes something you can't wait to share with others continually. The excitement is infectious.
"Page 11, **The "No Excuses" Mindset**

1- Farshad shared his experience of finding **hope** in his encounter with the lady that resulted in his first sale. Hope can be defined as a feeling of trust and expectation for a certain desire to happen or become true. Now based on this understanding, how could having hope be an important part of living a life with No Excuses?

2- Consider the "garbage in, garbage out" principle wherein the kinds of things we watch, listen to and think about represent our **mental diet**. How might your pathway to success be suffering as a result of your mental diet? Let's say you can transform GIGO into "good in, good out," will this exchange your suffering into success? If so, how?

3- Read how Farshad uses his vision board on pages 12-13. Who is the person you want to become in 3 years, 5 years and even 10 years from now?

4- A vision without a plan is nothing but a fantasy. What are the prices that you will need to pay in order to achieve your vision for the future? How badly do you really want it?

5- What situations bring out the best in you? When do you experience being fully engaged, energized and alive?

My 3D Mental Process

Vision: Do I have a crystal clear vision for what I want to do? Please explain.

_____
_____
_____
_____
_____
_____

Plan: What is my plan for accomplishing my vision? Is my daily agenda and activities in alignment with my objectives?

"This process of breaking the old habits and making new ones requires strategic planning. Your vision is your why, while your strategic plan is your how."
Page 14, **The "No Excuses" Mindset**

_____
_____
_____
_____
_____
_____

Outcome: How can I anticipate both positive and negative outcomes, and how can I learn to grow from them?

_____
_____
_____
_____
_____
_____

Chapter 1: In Plain Sight

My Massive Action Steps

1- _____
_____
_____
_____
_____
_____
_____
_____

I will complete this massive action step by (please list the dates):
_____

2- _____
_____
_____
_____
_____
_____
_____
_____

I will complete this massive action step by (please list the dates):
_____

3- _____
_____
_____
_____
_____
_____
_____
_____

I will complete this massive action step by: (please list the dates):
_____

Chapter 2 Agenda

Renovating the Mind

- Accountability Check
- Ice Breaker
- Round Table Talk
- My 3D Mental Process
- My Massive Action Steps

2. Renovating the Mind

"Most men would rather die than think. Many do."
Bertrand Russell

Ice Breaker

According to the study on page 30, when facing information that challenges their paradigm, only five percent of people were willing to think critically. In your opinion, why are so few people willing to think critically?

Round table topics

1- Why do you think people abandon their youthful curiosity?

2- In what ways has your thinking about success shifted throughout your life? What does success mean to you today?

3- Let's read Farshad's definition of commitment on page 29, "**Commitment** is not just trying, being interested, or promising that it will be done someday, sometime, or somewhere. The true definition of being committed is getting things done with absolutely **no excuses**, with an unshakable and undeniable **passion**, and un uncompromising **integrity**."

4- What value does this perspective on commitment hold for you?

5- Insight comes through reflection and represents the deepest level of knowing. How often do you take time to reflect? Are you willing to accept Farshad's challenge of intentionally practicing reflection **daily**?

6- How much time will you commit to reflection each day? When will you take the time to reflect each day?

"Reflection is an all-consuming, in-depth, and serious thought process that is required in a paradigm shift. Here lie the plains for consideration, contemplation, deliberation, meditation, rumination, and pondering – the quintessence of the 3D Mindset."
Page 31, **The "No Excuses" Mindset**

My 3D Mental Process

"Success is a personal matter and its variables depend on you. It is contingent on how often you think and reflect, how you implore your insight and explore a paradigm shift."
Page 33, **The "No Excuses" Mindset**

Vision: Am I allowing an old paradigm to cloud my vision? If so, how?

_____
_____
_____
_____
_____
_____
_____

Plan: Am I resistant to change? How can I plan to change for the better?

_____
_____
_____
_____
_____
_____
_____

Outcome: What would happen if I employed the four steps in this chapter?

1- Challenge Your Paradigm
2- Ask Questions
3- Be Open to Change
4- Take Decisive Action

How different will my life look in 1, 3, and 5 years?

_____
_____
_____
_____
_____
_____
_____

My Massive Action Steps

1- _____
_____
_____
_____
_____
_____
_____

I will complete this massive action step by (please list the dates):
_____

2- _____
_____
_____
_____
_____
_____
_____

I will complete this massive action step by (please list the dates):
_____

3- _____
_____
_____
_____
_____
_____
_____

I will complete this massive action step by: (please list the dates):
_____

Chapter 3 Agenda

Coaching

- Accountability Check
- Ice Breaker
- Round Table Talk
- My 3D Mental Process
- My Massive Action Steps

3. Coaching

"Rather than 'fixing' people, transformational coaches use problems to discover insights, intentions, and better ways of solving them." – Joan Goldsmith

Ice Breaker

Think of the teachers, mentors, and coaches who have added value to your life. Who among them stands out, and how did they add value to your life?

Round Table Topics

"Effective coaching builds awareness and removes the excuses. Coaching will help you replace those excuses and limiting beliefs with empowering dreams, and boost your self-confidence. Coaching can help you identify your values, discover your "why," set goals, increase self-esteem, and find a balance in life and business."
*Page 38, **The "No Excuses" Mindset***

1- Do you think that having a coach is essential for personal growth? In your perspective, what are the pros and cons of working with a coach?

2- Farshad recognized his father as a coach. Do you currently have anyone in your life that asks you great questions and supports you in living a life with no excuses? Who are they and how are they supporting you?

3- Coaches are not always professionals, therefore is it possible to suggest that anyone can step into the role of a coach? Have you ever stepped into this role? If so when? What was the outcome of your coaching? What worked, what didn't work?

4- What have you discovered in this chapter that will help you become a more effective coach?

5- Do you have a coach? How often do you meet? How effective has that been?

My 3D Mental Process

Note: If you don't think that you need a coach, consider the possibility that your vison is too small. Nothing significant has ever been accomplished by lone individuals. Expand your vison so that it can only be accomplished with the support of others.

Vision: Am I stuck in a rut? Do I need a coach to help me expand my vision? Why?

___

Plan: Who can I bring into my life tomorrow that will encourage me to live with no excuses? What connections am I making right now that I need to make better use of?

___

Outcome: Are the people I am surrounding myself with encouraging and uplifting me, or discouraging and bringing me down? How so?

___

My Massive Action Steps

1- _____

I will complete this massive action step by (please list the dates):

2- _____

I will complete this massive action step by (please list the dates):

3- _____

I will complete this massive action step by: (please list the dates):

Chapter 4 Agenda

Personal Growth

- Accountability Check
- Ice Breaker
- Round Table Talk
- My 3D Mental Process
- My Massive Action Steps

4. *No Excuses* - Personal Growth

*"The highest reward for a man's toil is not what he gets for it,
but what becomes by it." – Jon Ruskin*

Ice Breaker

Take a Moment to think of the people in your environment who have stopped growing. Maybe they have become jaded; maybe they don't think growth is important for them because they already know enough or they believe that they have done enough growing. In your perspective, where does it seem their lives are headed? What kind of relationships do they have? With whom do they surround themselves?

"Growth is only possible in an environment that is consistent, intentional, and positive."
Page 46, **The "No Excuses" Mindset**

Round table topics

"Personal growth doesn't occur without effort. The effort is one of recognizing your own power, and taking ownership and responsibility for your own development. This approach, the "No Excuses" way of acting and deciding, means that one no longer depend too heavily on others. It means taking charge of what you can change yourself." Page 49, **The "No Excuses" Mindset**

1- Why do you think that personal growth is important? Do you have a growth plan?

2- Farshad asserts that growth is not an event that happens in a day, but rather it is something that happens through the things we do daily, it becomes a habit. What are you doing daily to ensure that you continue to grow? (If you do not have a daily practice, what will you begin doing daily to ensure your continued growth?)

3- How has or will your continued growth positively influence the people around you?

4- Read Paula's story on page 50-51. By committing to her personal growth, Paula created a positive energy loop that affected all aspects of her life. How was your personal commitment to personal growth affected the other aspects of your life?

5- A No Excuses mindset is something that we must grow into, in fact, it occurs as a direct result of personal growth. What is/are the area(s) of your life where you need to grow the most?

My 3D Mental Process

"The 'No Excuses' mindset is at its core the clear result of a 'Personal Growth' habit. Personal growth will make all the other areas seem a bit less challenging and it will put you one step closer to living with 'No Excuses.'"
*Page 54, **The "No Excuses" Mindset***

Vision: What excuses am I making for delaying or ignoring my own personal growth? How do I see my own development over the next several years?

_____
_____
_____
_____
_____
_____

Plan: What steps do I need to take in order to improve myself? How do I need to rearrange my schedule in order to better my personal goals?

_____
_____
_____
_____
_____
_____

Outcome: In what ways could personal growth free up my time and make me more valuable to others?

_____
_____
_____
_____
_____
_____

My Massive Action Steps

1- _____
_____
_____
_____
_____
_____
_____
_____

I will complete this massive action step by (please list the dates):
_____

2- _____
_____
_____
_____
_____
_____
_____
_____

I will complete this massive action step by (please list the dates):
_____

3- _____
_____
_____
_____
_____
_____
_____
_____

I will complete this massive action step by: (please list the dates):
_____

Chapter 5 Agenda

Relationships

- Accountability Check
- Ice Breaker
- Round Table Talk
- My 3D Mental Process
- My Massive Action Steps

5. *No Excuses* - Relationships

"Any conception of the good life (except to the rare hermit or lone mountaineer) that leaves out the importance of human relationships is pathetic and unrealistic."
– Fernando Flores

Ice Breaker

According to Farshad, there are generally three kinds of people: those who **lean**, those who **lift**, and those who **lead**. What kind of person are you, leaner, lifter, or leader?

"People who lean immobilize you; stay away from them. People who lift inspire you; keep them near. People who lead positively influence you; seek them out."
Page 58 **The "No Excuses" Mindset**

Round Table Topics

"It is through our contact with others on a daily basis that we acquire knowledge, learn skills, develop our goals, and capture the chance at a better future. Meeting one person can unlock possibilities we never knew existed. Unfortunately,... We create excuse that stand between us and other people; excuses that separate us from the happiness and the prospects these people can present."
Page 57, **The "No Excuses" Mindset**

1- What are the consequences of lacking personal connection in today's world?

2- Why do you think face-to-face engagement is essential for personal growth?

3- Solid relationships require investments of quality time and energy. Take a moment to reflect on the relationships in which you have decided to invest. In which relationships are you investing in the most?

4- If you died today, how would your best friend eulogize you? What kind of impact would people say that you made within your community?

My 3D Mental Process

"Developing strong interpersonal relationships by creating lasting connections instead of just passing acquaintances will take your life and business to a new level."
Page 63, ***The "No Excuses" Mindset***

Vision: What value will I find and give in my day to day relationships with others?

_____
_____
_____
_____
_____
_____

Plan: How can I relate better to others? What steps can I take to invest in people's lives?

_____
_____
_____
_____
_____
_____

Outcome: What will my life look like when I invest in my relationships? Please provide some examples.

_____
_____
_____
_____
_____
_____

My Massive Action Steps

1- _____
_____
_____
_____
_____
_____
_____

I will complete this massive action step by (please list the dates):
_____

2- _____
_____
_____
_____
_____
_____
_____

I will complete this massive action step by (please list the dates):
_____

3- _____
_____
_____
_____
_____
_____
_____

I will complete this massive action step by: (please list the dates):
_____

Chapter 6 Agenda

Family

- Accountability Check
- Ice Breaker
- Round Table Talk
- My 3D Mental Process
- My Massive Action Steps

6. *No Excuses* - Family

"The way you help heal the world is you start with your own family."
– Mother Teresa

Ice Breaker

What does family mean to you?

Round table Topics

> *"A 'No Excuses' mindset in your family stems directly from your personal growth. If you are not growing as a person, the first impact will affect your family."*
> Page 72, **The "No Excuses" Mindset**

1. Our personal growth affects all areas of our lives. How has your commitment to personal growth impacted your family?

2. What are the ways in which your family adds value to your life?

3. In what ways are you adding value to the lives of your family members?

4. What healing needs to take place within your family?

> *"It is in the home that the rough edges show and new areas of shortcoming surface; that gives more occasion for personal growth to take place in the home than in any other environment."*
> Page 73 **The "No Excuses" Mindset**

Continued Round Table Topics (optional)

1. What are some of the lingering issues you still have with your family (parents, spouse, kids…)?

2. How often do you have a date night with your spouse or significant other?

3. How comfortable are you with having open honest communication with your family in real time?

4. Are you able to turn your family's or personal mistakes into teachable moments and lessons?

Farshad Asl

My 3D Mental Process

*"Because family and friends are the foundation of who you are,
this is a realm where no excuses should exist. Give them your al without excuses."*
Page 76 **The "No Excuses" Mindset**

Vision: What are the characteristics I would like to see developed in my family? What are some of the traditions I want to bring with them?

_____
_____
_____
_____
_____
_____

Plan: What needs to change in my life to bring health and wholeness to my family? How can I model a *No Excuses* mindset for my spouse, children, and family?

_____
_____
_____
_____
_____
_____

Outcome: If I maintain the status quo, where will it take my family? Will we grow closer together or further apart? (Please provide some examples.)

_____
_____
_____
_____
_____
_____

Chapter 6: Family

My Massive Action Steps

1- _____

_____

_____

_____

_____

_____

_____

I will complete this massive action step by (please list the dates):

_____

2- _____

_____

_____

_____

_____

_____

_____

I will complete this massive action step by (please list the dates):

_____

3- _____

_____

_____

_____

_____

_____

_____

I will complete this massive action step by: (please list the dates):

_____

TOPLeaders

Chapter 7 Agenda

Business

- Accountability Check
- Ice Breaker
- Round Table Talk
- My 3D Mental Process
- My Massive Action Steps

7. *No Excuses* - Business

"Greatness is not a function of circumstances. Greatness, it turns out, is largely a matter of conscious choice." -Jim Collins

Ice Breaker

We all have greatness within us. What is the job, career, or service you could be great at? What is your area of greatness?

Round Table Topics

"Your crystal clear vision should provide you a glimpse of the new universe and should have turned your excuses for failure into purpose for progress. The shallowness of your previous failures has become a deep well of resources for success."
Page 86 **The "No Excuses" Mindset**

1- In your perspective, how would a *No Excuses* mindset provide an edge for people in their careers?

2- What are you investing your energy in? Is it something you can be great at? Please explain.

3- What would an investment in yourself look like? Please provide examples.

4- What is your dream project that you have been procrastinating on for days, months, or even years? What is holding you back?

5- If you knew you could not fail, what would you do for a living?

My 3D Mental Process

"Successful entrepreneurs don't have better ideas; instead they have better mindsets for taking action. Action is what sets apart an aspiring entrepreneur from others."
Page 92, **The "No Excuses" Mindset**

Vision: What career opportunities am I missing out on by holding on to my excuses? Do I envision myself in the same place for the rest of my life?

_____
_____
_____
_____
_____
_____
_____

Plan: How can I invest in myself today in order to prepare for the future? What steps can I take to "get unstuck" from my current situation?

_____
_____
_____
_____
_____
_____
_____

Outcome: Am I content where I am? What would my career look like if I quit making excuses, start providing solutions, and used my creativity?

_____
_____
_____
_____
_____
_____
_____

Chapter 7: Business

My Massive Action Steps

1- _____
_____
_____
_____
_____
_____
_____

I will complete this massive action step by (please list the dates):
_____

2- _____
_____
_____
_____
_____
_____
_____

I will complete this massive action step by (please list the dates):
_____

3- _____
_____
_____
_____
_____
_____
_____

I will complete this massive action step by: (please list the dates):
_____

Chapter 8 Agenda

Legacy

- Accountability Check
- Ice Breaker
- Round Table Talk
- My 3D Mental Process
- My Massive Action Steps

8. *No Excuses* - Legacy

"Carve your name on hearts, not tombstones. A legacy is etched into the minds of others and the stories they share about you." – Shannon L. Alder

Ice Breaker

"A legacy is the impact and impression an individual makes and leaves behind in the lives of others; it no longer represents the individual, it represents the people who carry on his or her name with passion and integrity."
Page 99, **The "No Excuses" Mindset**

When you think about legacy, who or what is the first person that comes to your mind? Why?

Round Table Topics:

The legacy we leave is not just in our possessions but in the quality of our lives.
– Billy Graham

1- What comes to mind when you think about the legacy that you want to leave behind?

2- If you found out today that you have a terminal illness, how would you change the way you live your life?

3- Take a moment to think about your life. What is the legacy that only you have the potential to fulfill?

4- Imagine your 85th birthday party and all the people you care about are there to offer you encouraging words. What would you hope to hear from them? In what ways will they say that you have added value to their lives by serving and loving them?

Round Table Topics Continued (optional)

1- What do I want to be known for?

2- What are my top three core values?

3- Am I living in a way that represents those values?

My 3D Mental Process

"Everyone leaves behind a legacy of some kind, but those who approaching living with a 'No Excuses' mindset leave a legacy of value. A life hidden behind the veil of excuses leaves behind a blank page, but a life with the brilliant light of purpose shone upon it fills every page with wisdom." Page 109 **The "No Excuses" Mindset**

Vision: Do I live my life to the fullest? Do I live a life of success or a life of significance? (Please explain)

_____
_____
_____
_____
_____
_____

Plan: How can I love the people around me? How can I leave something worthwhile behind? If I should pass away unexpectedly, can I leave this life with no regrets? Am I ready to go?

_____
_____
_____
_____
_____
_____

Outcome: What would happen if I lived a life of significance? If I had a little more time, what would I change? Am I ready to leave my legacy?

_____
_____
_____
_____
_____
_____

My Massive Action Steps

1- _____

I will complete this massive action step by (please list the dates):

2- _____

I will complete this massive action step by (please list the dates):

3- _____

I will complete this massive action step by: (please list the dates):

Farshad's Mission Statement:

> "Developing leaders who inspire leadership in others, leaving a legacy of impacting the lives of people we touch with passion and integrity."

"There are some values that you should never compromise on to stay true to yourself; you should be brave to stand up for what you truly believe in even if you stand alone."
— *Roy T. Bennett*

Farshad's Core Values:

Faith/Family Passion Integrity	Serving Others Accomplishments Legacy

P.O.S.I.T.I.V.E. GOALS™

"We are living in an era of constant evolution and development. It is a time of rapid transformations, inventions, and breakthroughs. If we desire to stay current then our goals and goal setting skills need to be revamped and become applicable to our time."
Page 46, ***The "No Excuses" Mindset***

Living life with the *"No Excuses"* mindset not only requires a transformation of our minds, but also a transformation in our actions. Spend a few minutes reflecting on the following questions. Once you have found clarity in your personal growth throughout this mastermind journey, move on to setting your **P.O.S.I.T.I.V.E Goals™**.

- **Has your vision for life become crystal clear (20/20)?**
- **Have your plans become strategic and filled with significance?**
- **Have your outcomes become measurable with value?**

*"...now is the time to shift the paradigm. There needs to be a new platform with a new purpose for effective and modern goal setting that will expand potential, accomplish things beyond imagination and achieve extraordinary results. It is time to set **P.O.S.I.T.I.V.E Goals™**."*
Page 47, ***The "No Excuses" Mindset***

P.O.S.I.T.I.V.E. GOAL™ SETTING WORKSHEET

NAME _____ DATE _____

P. Passionate: A P.O.S.I.T.I.V.E. goal is driven by passion. It fires you up and fuels your days with purpose, enthusiasm, and excitement. Your goal becomes pivotal to your daily exercises. It will create that burning desire within to bring your goal into reality. A goal that is fueled with passion will never burn out; it will only thrive.

O. Outside the box: A P.O.S.I.T.I.V.E. goal should not bound by a criterion. It is not measured, limited, or simplified. Your goal pushes you out of your comfort zone and dares you to take risks. A P.O.S.I.T.I.V.E. goal gives you courage and enables your creativity. It will take beyond the realm of expectation and imagination. Your goal is a manifestation of your wildest dreams; you wouldn't box up your dreams, right?

S. Significant: A P.O.S.I.T.I.V.E. goal enriches and benefits the lives of others and adds value to everyone and everything on its course. Your goal will create a win-win situation at any cost. The traces of significance that are left behind in the lives of others by your goal are as important as its fruition; for that too is its manifestation.

I. Innovative: A P.O.S.I.T.I.V.E. goal delineates between opportunities and challenges to creatively reach and surpass any hindrance en route its success. Your goal is constantly raising the bar and is exponentially growing. An innovative goal is bigger, better, and bolder.

T. Time-sensitive: A P.O.S.I.T.I.V.E. goal requires a sense of urgency. This is the key to achieving great results. Your goal will have a tremendous momentum that will fuel everything you do, because all things should work together towards its fruition. With a time sensitive mindset you can hit and exceed your goals.

I. Impactful: A P.O.S.I.T.I.V.E. goal empowers, influences, and encourages. It is positive in intention, direction, and outcome. Your goal takes into account all the players of the game and all steps taken with purpose. With the right intentions, your goal will make an impact and a difference.

V. Visionary: A P.O.S.I.T.I.V.E. goal is multifaceted. Your goal belongs to a bigger whole. It is piece of a larger impact. With a clear vision, your goal can identify and look beyond any limits or restrictions. It takes a visionary to recognize the true reality of his goal.

E. Evolving: A P.O.S.I.T.I.V.E. goal not only focuses on its final purpose but also in its process towards fruition. Your goal will help you develop new skills to achieve significant results. Setting a positive goal is embarking on a journey of transformation. As you shift the paradigm of goal setting and you evolve yourself. The destination of your goal will be evolutionary.

"Set your objectives high, and don't stop till you get there. It's time to make your dream a reality. It's your time to live your dream. LET'S GO!" ~Farshad Asl

1. What is your 5-year P.O.S.I.T.I.V.E. Goal? (Reference the acronym, be specific, be detailed, and be courageous. Imagine big and imagine wild.)

   _____
   _____
   _____
   _____
   _____

2. What is your short-term P.O.S.I.T.I.V.E. Goal? (Goal for the upcoming year. This goal will be your first step towards your 5-year Goal.)

   _____
   _____
   _____
   _____
   _____

3. Why is *this* your goal? What is your purpose and passion? (Knowing your WHY will give you your HOW.)

   _____
   _____
   _____
   _____
   _____

4. Is your Goal crystal clear? Will you be able to describe it to a complete stranger in one sentence?

   YES or NO? (Circle one)

5. Who are you going to become with this goal? How will you evolve? Who will you impact?

   _____
   _____
   _____
   _____
   _____

Farshad Asl

6. What skills, abilities, and/or resources will your goal require you to have?

_____

_____

_____

_____

_____

7. Is your Goal…? (Circle all that apply)

                Passionate

                Out of the Box

                Significant

                Innovative

                Time-sensitive

                Impactful

                Visionary

                Evolving

*"Create an environment to grow consistently and to impact everyone around you positively. Today is a NEW day! Your future doesn't have to equal your past. You are designed to achieve greatness, to be happy and to live the life you deserve. Start with setting **P.O.S.I.T.I.V.E. Goals™.**"*
Page 49 The "No Excuses" Mindset

Congratulations on completing the *No Excuses* Mastermind!

- Make sure you collect your signed certificate of completion from your mastermind team leader.

- You are now a part of the **No Excuses Mindset** family 20/20.

- With your completion of this mastermind, you are now exclusively a part of the **Top Leaders Academy**. Complementary to you, please register at TopLeaders.co

- Now that you are a part of this worldwide family, you will have access to ongoing support through the following sources:

TOP Leaders

- Topleaders.co
- Topleadersnews.com

- Facebook.com/topleaders
- Linkedin.com/farshadasl
- Twitter @topleadersco
- Email us at TopleadersInc@outlook.com and ask about the Top Leaders Academy.

FARSHAD ASL
LIVE WITH PASSION

For a Life-Changing Experience

Invite Farshad Asl to speak at your next event.

Author, Entrepreneur, Leadership Coach, International Speaker, & Regional Director of Sales for Bankers Life

ARE YOU READY TO EXCHANGE EXCUSES FOR EXCELLENCE? Does your business, organization, or community need a new mindset? Are you overdue for a paradigm shift? Are you ready to learn an innovative way to overcome life's challenges? If so, then Farshad Asl will exceed your expectations. It's time you became the person you are destined to be.

Live a life of passion, purpose and clarity with "No Excuses."

Reach Farshad Asl at:

TopLeaders.co

FARSHAD ASL
LIVE WITH PASSION

Live a life of passion, purpose and clarity with *"No Excuses."*

"There are life stories and then there are stories that change lives. *The "No Excuses" Mindset* is filled with real life stories that will change your life. This will be a book you will want to use as a guide as you live out your own life story."

—**Paul Martinelli, President The John Maxwell Team**

"Farshad is a leader who sets high standards for himself as a leader and that is the secret to his success. In *The "No Excuses" Mindset* he shares with us the ways we can take decisive actions, providing us with a new landscape of opportunity in how we live our lives and lead our business."

—**Deb Ingino, CEO Strength Leader Development**

"With compelling candor and masterful storytelling, Farshad Asl serves us rich content forged from his proven process. *The "No Excuses" Mindset* opened me up to what's possible personally and professionally."

—**Kary Oberbrunner, Author of Day Job to Dream Job, The Deeper Path, Your Secret Name, and ELIXIR Project**

"Everyone should read this excellent book to develop a *"No Excuses"* mindset. You'll be inspired by Farshad's life story and others who are testaments to applying a 3D Mindset. These practical ideas will dramatically impact your business, professional success, personal life and family."

—**Mike Esterday, CEO, Integrity Solutions**

"*The "No Excuses" Mindset* is a book about purpose, passion and perseverance. It explains the journey of every successful person who dared to follow their dream. Farshad not only shows you his journey to achieving his dream; he has created a roadmap to enable you to achieve yours!"

—**Johnny Walker, MA, CPC, Founder, Foundational Core Values™**

"This book is a gift to anyone who reads it. Farshad Asl lives this message, making this book an inspirational and practical handbook for eliminating the excuses that would hold you back. In fact, as you read these pages you will not only be stripped from the excuses you've relied on but some new ones will be revealed. I dare you to begin at once!"

—**Scott M. Fay, Vice President, The John Maxwell Team**

Reach Farshad Asl at:

TopLeaders.co

Made in the USA
Las Vegas, NV
19 March 2025